Irish Crochet Lace

Irish Crochet Lace

Motifs from County Monaghan, collected and described by
Eithne d'Arcy

with photographs by John-David Biggs

The Dolmen Press

Irish Crochet Lace by Eithne d'Arcy is set in Paladium
type and printed in the Republic of Ireland by
Irish Printers Ltd. for the publishers,

The Dolmen Press Limited
Mountrath
Portlaoise
Ireland.

Designed by Liam Miller.
Typesetting and page assembly by Computer Graphics Ltd.
Photography by John-David Biggs.

First published 1984.

British Library Cataloguing in Publication Data

d'Arcy, Eithne
Irish crochet lace
1. Crocheting - patterns
746.43'4041 TT820
ISBN 0 85105 421 8

Contents

Foreword

Irish Crochet Lace records the steps in lacemaking through simple instructions and photographic illustrations, which are reproduced larger than actual size so that each step is clearly detailed for the lacemaker. As the foundation step in each motif governs the finished size, the worker can plan the desired finished size of a pattern. The number of stitches given for each motif here is stated only to establish the size. One must remember that the old workers did not count their stitches but relied on visual expertise, which they acquired at an early age.

The original pieces inherited by Eithne d'Arcy and illustrated here were worked in fine Manloves linen thread, which is no longer available. While the beauty of these old pieces is enhanced by the use of this linen thread, the motifs described in this book display the lasting beauty of the craft, even if worked in coarse crochet cotton. The motifs described can also be worked in silk.

Eithne d'Arcy still visits the few remaining lacemakers near her home. Her life has been lived surrounded by lace and embroidery and her labour of the last three years, spent compiling this book, has been a joy to her. She worked each step in the patterns herself to be photographed for the book. If her 'labour of love' helps to revive this craft in which Irish women and girls excelled, she will be happy that her efforts have succeeded.

Introduction

Of all the forms of crochet lace, that known as 'Irish Crochet' is the most sought after and is probably the best known. It was regarded by the couture profession in the early years of this century as the true Irish lace. While the Irish tradition for producing this work dates back to the sixteenth century, when it was known as 'nun's work' because the technique and style of the craft was developed in Irish convent communities in imitation of continental European lacemaking styles, the manufacture of crochet lace did not become a cottage industry in Ireland until the middle of the nineteenth century.

The inventor of the style of crochet which is the subject of *Irish Crochet Lace* was Mademoiselle Riego de la Blanchardaire, who discovered that a type of Spanish Needlepoint could effectively be adapted to Irish materials.

During the famine years of the 1840's the Ursuline Sisters established 'Crochet centres' in Ireland, the first in 1845 in their convent at Blackrock in County Cork, to help relieve starvation in the neighbourhood. Crochet-making was soon adopted by many other centres throughout the country. And so crochet, which originally had been deemed 'nun's work' in the convents of Europe or was the prerogative of the manor, changed and developed a unique style, which became, for Irish people, a symbol of life, hope and pride. In the years immediately after the famine, crochet became a practical subject in the curriculum of convent schools. The crochet lace developed in Irish convents had a rich and decorative appearance which was partly due to the nuns' adaptation of motifs from seventeenth century Venetian needlepoint, as well as from the then fashionable Honiton lace from England and the Flemish lace, Mechelen. So attractive was this new crochet that from about 1850 it was sought by the fashion conscious in Paris, Vienna, Brussels, London and New York.

Cork was soon recognized as the main centre of the crochet lace industry in the South of Ireland but the manufacture soon spread to other areas. Mrs W. C. Thornton introduced crochet as an experiment in County Kildare, first as a famine relief scheme, and it proved so successful that a demand developed for teachers to go to other parts of Ireland. The Rector's wife at Clones in County Monaghan, Mrs Cassandra Hand, invited one of these teachers to her area. The combination of Mrs Hand's business ability and the expertise of the teacher soon made Clones one of the principal centres of the craft. Exquisite models of Guipure and Point de Venise lace were developed there and Mrs Hand also developed a style of crochet based on Church lace, which became available after the dissolution of the monasteries in Spain. Within a few years of the establishment of the Clones school in 1847, about fifteen hundred workers were employed

Introduction

directly or indirectly through crochet working in the parish. As a result, by 1910, Clones was the most important centre of the industry in Ireland.

At the time that Clones lace was in demand, the standard of living in Ireland was very poor. In this depressed economic period, lacemaking provided a very important contribution to the budgets of families whose women had the skill. The fashions of the time created a great demand for lace for blouse bodices and cuffs, ruffles, trimmings and even whole dresses. Men wore lace in the form of jabots and evening shirts. New motifs were added by the workers themselves so that Clones lace eventually became an art form native to Clones and the surrounding area.

Irish crochet became popular in the 1850's, a time when ornate machine made lace was becoming readily available. The result was a period of general decline in the development of the craft. By the late nineteenth century there was a change in fashion and lace was again favoured. Encouragement from state and charitable organisations helped to bring Irish crochet back to its position of renown as Ireland's most distinctive 'lace'. By 1904, Paris couturiers were using Irish crochet lace in their summer creations and Irish crochet was soon in demand in the other fashion centres of the world.

After the First World War fashion became less feminine, employing other fabrics than lace, which needed care in its upkeep, and those decades saw a decline in interest. Fortunately today, there is a greater appreciation of hand-made fabrics and the support of the Irish Countrywomen's Association, The Royal Dublin Society, the Vocational Education Committees and the Irish Lace Guild have ensured a revival of interest in Irish crochet lace.

Clones Crochet Lace

Some examples from the author's collection

Illustrations 1-7 are examples of the work of the late Mrs Mulligan of Killyliffer, Roslea, County Fermanagh. Her maiden name was McCarron and she lived for many years in Clones.

1 Small round piece

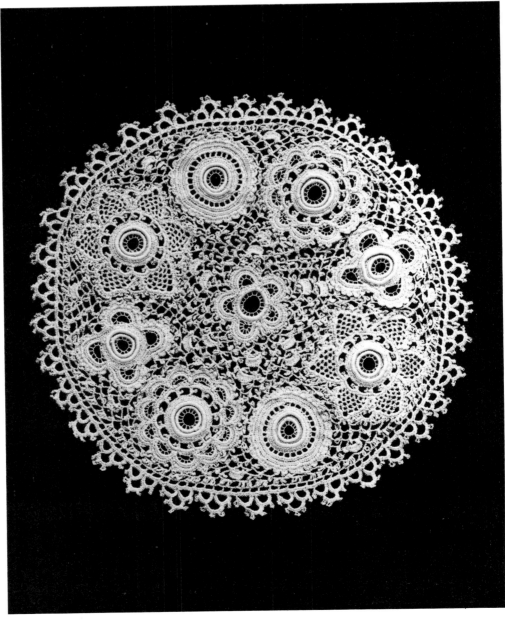

3   Large round piece

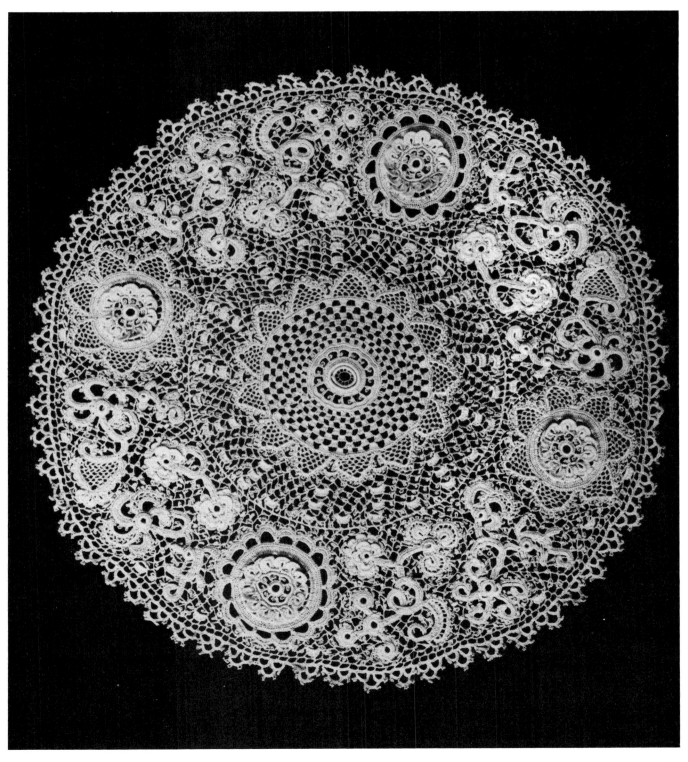

4 Small round piece
5 Small round piece

6   Small rectangular piece

7   Small rectangular piece

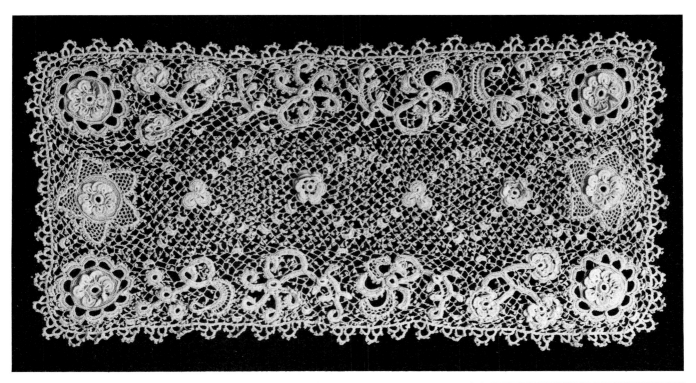

8   Old crochet collar (Worker unknown). The round collar shows how the traditional lacemakers worked mitres easily by using a rose motif (6) and a small version of the shamrock spray (23). Fine squares with rose hearts form the centre of this collar and blend with the motifs. The piece is 60-70 years old.

9   Small jabot
Three small squares complete with edging and joined at three corners form a simple jabot for a dress front.

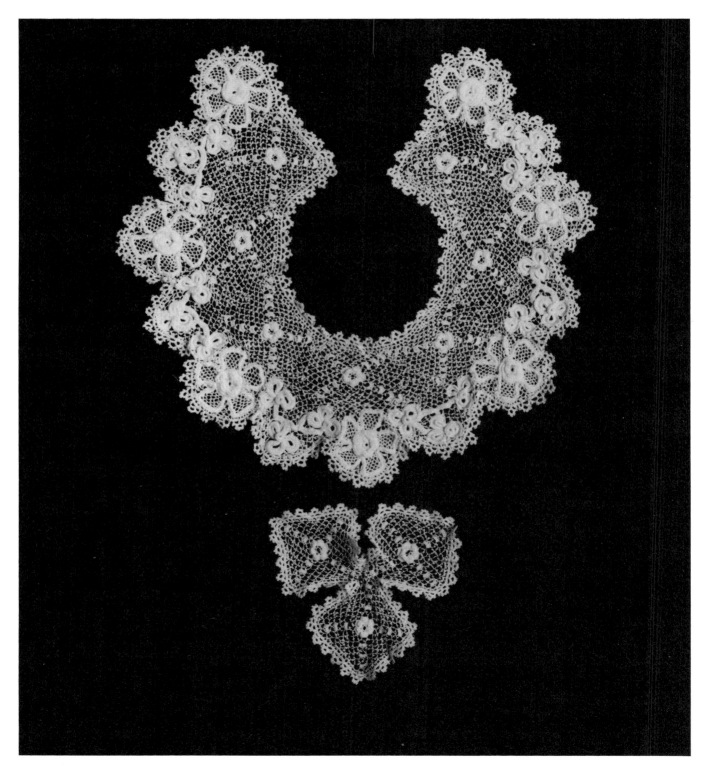

10 Old Clones lace worked in silk thread.
It is not known who worked this piece, nor
its age.

11 Old tea cosy (Worker unknown)
This piece is worked in a fine linen probably the Manloves linen crochet thread which was specially made for Clones work. The Clones knot and a variety of sprays make up the design. The piece is between sixty and seventy years old. Different motifs are used on both sides of the tea cosy.

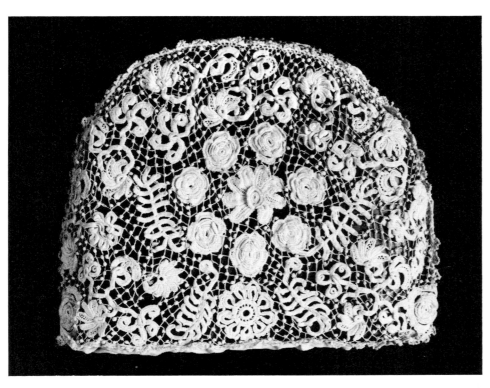

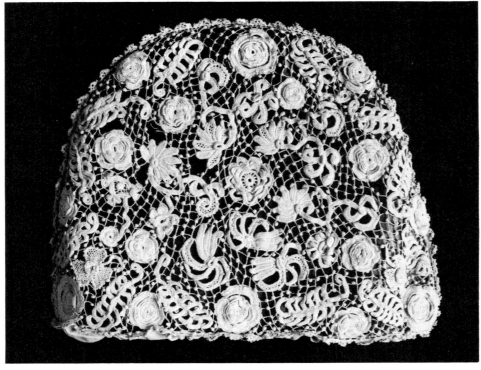

12 Large rectangular piece.
This design incorporates a slightly enlarged
rose with a fern motif. It shows how
individual workers created their own
designs for special orders.

13, 14.   A lunch set, worked by the late
Mrs M. Boyle of Bunnablaneybane,
Roslea, between forty and fifty years ago.

Crochet Lace Materials and Technique

The technique of Irish crochet lace (Clones Lace) as described in this book is significantly different from other lacemaking techniques. The lacemaker has considerable freedom in the arrangement of the motifs in a design and can adapt any design to a personal preference.

Materials:
Cotton, Linen Thread, Silk, Mercerised Cotton.
Hook: 0.75
Cord: 1, 2, 3 or 4 pieces of Cotton folded.
Tension:
Fairly tight throughout.

The illustrations in this book are not actual size, but have been enlarged to help the lacemaker to follow the detail of the work.

Pattern: A foundation pattern is prepared in the desired design (e.g. for a blouse, a dress yoke, a nightdress yoke, a table mat, a cushion cover or a curtain). The old lacemakers usually used a brown paper pattern. I suggest that a backing of lightweight fabric should be attached to the brown paper pattern for ease of working. The motifs are arranged over this foundation and tacked down before they are joined by the chosen filling.

Motifs: The motifs — flowers, leaves and sprays — are worked over a core of padding cord or thread, formed from two, three or four strands of cotton. The cord is a very important element in the lace as the shapes of the motifs can be adjusted by altering the tension of the cord. The degree of tightening or loosening of the cord will be learned by experience.

Joining: When making something large, for example a blouse, one should work a long chain with:— seven chain, four chain picot, seven chain, four chain picot. This is then sewn around the edge of the pattern and acts as a joining stitch when you come to the end of a row. No turnings are required as the joining stitch is seven chain, four chain picot, three chain, double crochet in the corresponding opposite stitch. When the joining stitch is complete, the threads at the back material side may be cut easily without damaging your lace.

Fillings: When working the filling between motifs, it is best to use a coarser thread. If the motifs themselves are worked with number forty crochet cotton, the joining may be worked with number twenty or number thirty crochet of the same make. This is a method which I have devised and differs from the techniques of the old lacemakers.

There are several forms of filling patterns, — plain, picot, double picot, Clones knot etc. The lacemaker will use her experience in determining the style and filling used in a pattern. It is important however that the motifs do not come too near the edge as this might interfere with the edge pattern. It is also essential that the work be kept flat while the filling is being worked. While the types of thread used may vary, the lacemaker should always use the finest hook possible. Irish lace looks best when worked with firm, fairly tight tension. In this book, the motifs are worked over a core of padding thread, formed from two, three or four strands of cotton (usually number ten cotton) and it is important, when working over this padding thread, that each thread is tightened seperately because if all the strands are pulled together, one may become wrinkled.

The stitches used in this book are simple crochet stitches: chain stitch (ch. st.); slip stitch (ss.); double crochet (dc.); half treble (h.tr.); treble (tr.) and double treble (d.tr.). Each stitch should be practiced individually before a complete motif is attempted and the worker should practice the required motifs before attempting a complete pattern.

To crochet a pattern the required motifs should be worked first. If the motifs become soiled, they may be washed individually by hand and while still damp, may be eased gently back into shape, placed face down on a soft flannel and, using a damp flannel cover for protection, pressed gently with a medium hot iron. The motifs should then be left overnight in a cool room before being placed on the pattern.

When work is complete a straight row is worked, usually this is 3ch double crochet in required space or if necessary treble crochet in required space. Stitches used here must be judged by the worker.

Abbreviations used

ch	chain.
ss	slip stitch.
st(s)	stitch(es).
dc	double crochet.
tr	treble.
dtr	double treble.
htr	half treble.
sp	space.
p	picot.
lp(s)	loop(s).
beg.	beginning.
w/c	wind cord.
t/c	tighten cord.
l/c	leave cord.
b/i/c	bring in cord.
Fasten off	neatly fasten off cotton and cord.
k/n	knitting needle.

AMERICAN CROCHET TERMS

Although the stitches used in American crochet are identical to those used in Ireland, some of them have different names: viz

Irish		American	
double crochet	dc	single crochet	sc
treble	tr	double crochet	dc
double treble	dtr	treble	tr
Half treble	htr	half double	hdc

Example: The Clones Knot

Steps 1 & 2. 7 ch. Thread over needle.

Steps 3, 4, 5 & 6. Bring thread around under ch. Thread round hook. Return to position 2. Repeat 9 times.

Steps 7 & 8. Draw 9th loop through all loops on hook. Fasten with slp. st. to 6th of 7 ch. 6 ch. Join to required loop of previous row. Continue to end of row.

When working second and subsequent rows, work 1 dc on each side of knot, keeping knot to front of work.

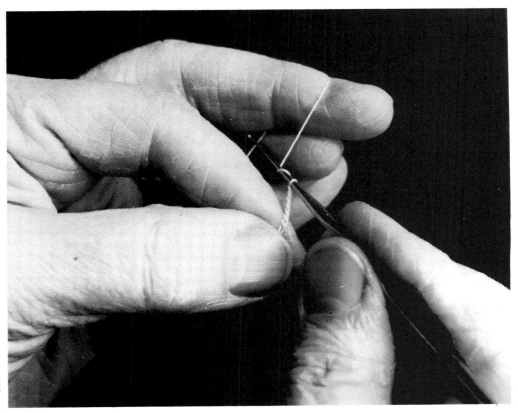

Bringing the thread round under the needle (step 2).

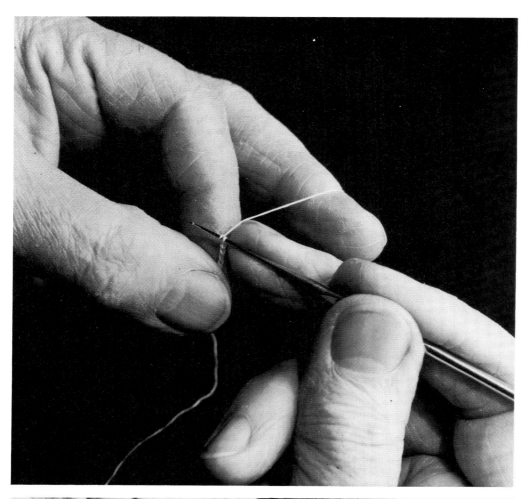

Thread round hook, catch up in a loop.

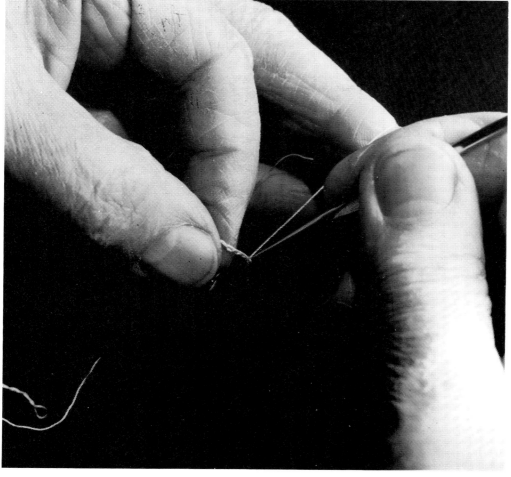

Twist the needle round the thread, an 'under and under' movement.

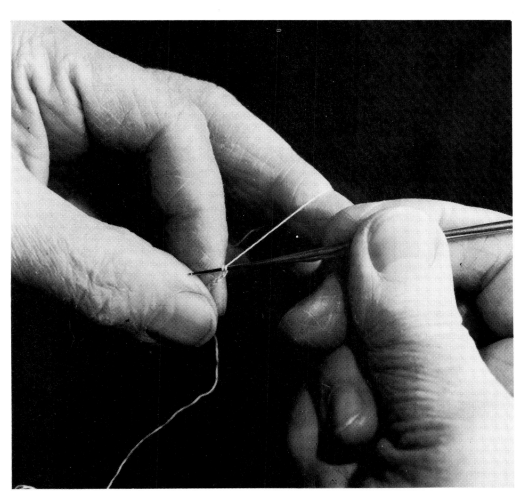

Bring the needle back to first position.

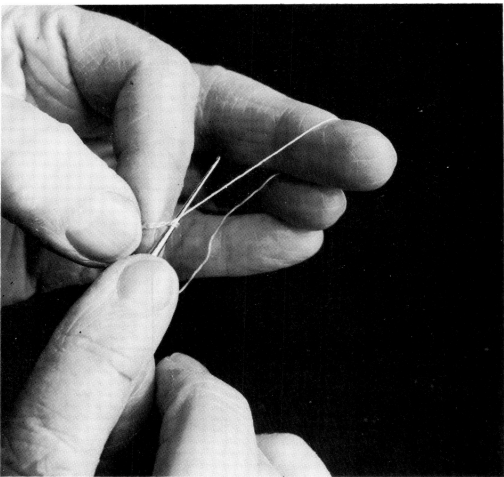

Bring the needle round under cotton make another loop on the needle.

27

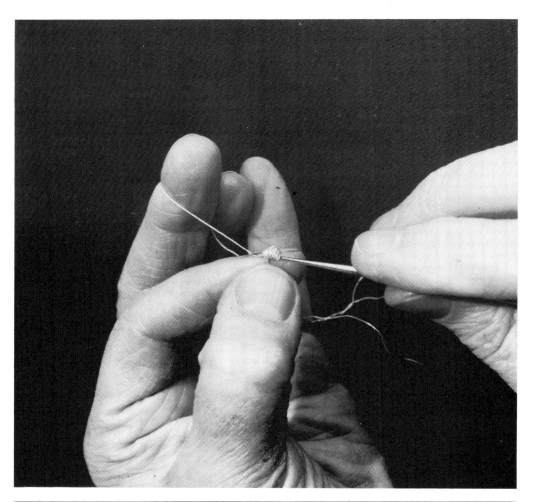

Bring the thread round the needle hook.

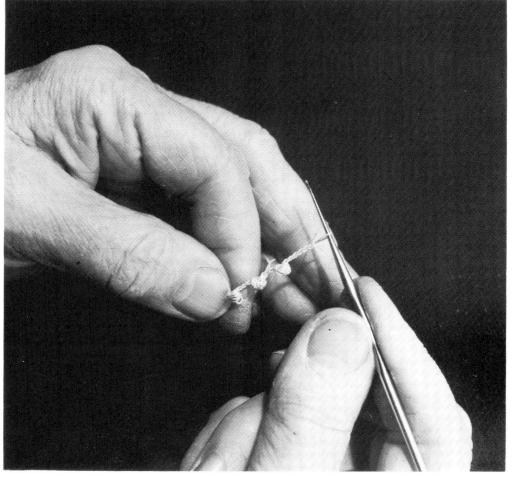

Working 7 chain and Clones knot along the place required. When working the next row, work 7 chain, Clones knot, 7 chain, work round the back of the knot on the previous row to make each knot sit up well.

Motif 1: Nine-Looped Flower

Materials:
No. 0.75 Crochet Hook.
Approx. 15" 2-Strand Padding Cord.
No. 40 Crochet Cotton.
Approx. 6" 2-Strand Padding Cord.

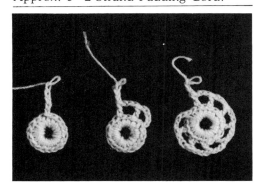

Step 1. Wind cotton 10 times round No. 10 k/n. Slip off needle, work 2 ch, 17 dc into ring, ss to 2 ch.

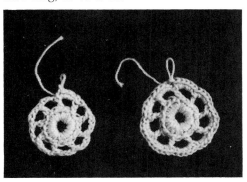

Step 2. 5 ch, miss 1 dc, 1 tr in next dc, (3 ch, miss 1 dc, 1 tr in next dc,) 8 times, only on last 3 ch ss. to 2nd of 5 ch. (9 lps) 1 ch, 4 dc in 1st 3 ch lp, 5 dc in 2nd and each following lp. ss to 1 ch.

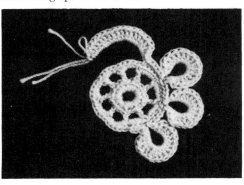

Step 3. B/i/p/c, over p/c work 1 dc in each next 4 dc. ** Over p/c only work 1 dc, 1 hlf tr, 15tr, 1 hlf tr, 1 dc, ss to 4th dc, t/p/c to form a neat loop, 1 dc in each next 5 dc **. Repeat from ** to ** 8 more times. ss to 1 ch. Fasten off p/c and cotton neatly. (9 loops).

Step 4. Fasten 2 strands of p/c to 7th st at side of any lp. (approx 6" 2-Strand p/c) 1 dc, 1 hlf tr, 1 tr, 1 hlf tr, 1 dc, ss to 10th st on lp. 1 dc, 1 hlf tr, 1 tr, 1 dc, ss to 13th st on lp. 1 dc on p/c only, (5 times) ss to 7th st on next lp. Repeat this step on each lp. t/p/c. Fasten off neatly.

Motif 2: Half Scroll

Materials:
No. 4 Crochet Hook.
4 Strand p/c, 12″.
No. 40 Cotton.

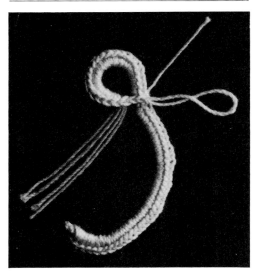

Step 1. Over 4 p/c, work 60 dc, 1 ch, ss to 24th dc from hook to form a ring at one end, t/c, 1 ch turn.

Steps 2. & 3. Continue over p/c, work 1 dc in each dc on ring, 1 hlf tr in next dc, 1 tr in each following dc, only in 1st 2 dc work 1 hlf tr, 1 dc, 3 dc on p/c only turn. t/c to form a curve. Fasten off p/c neatly.

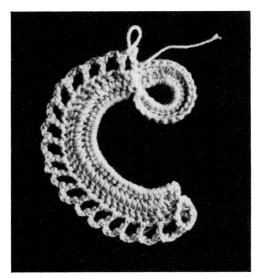

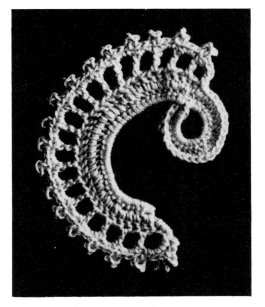

Step 4. Miss 1 st, 1 tr in next st, ** 3 ch, miss 1 st 1 tr in next st, repeat from ** to last dc, work 1 hlf tr in last dc on ring. Turn.

Step 5. 3 dc into 1st 3 ch, 4 ch p, repeat to end of row.

Motif 3: Dahlia

Materials:
No. 0.75 Crochet Hook
No Padding Cord.
No. 40 Crochet Cotton.

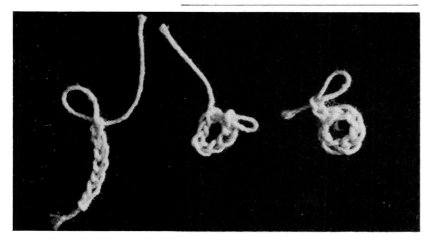

Steps 1, 2 & 3. Begin with 6 ch, ss to 1st ch to form ring. 2 ch.

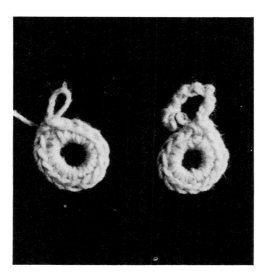

Steps 4 & 5. 14 dc into ring, ss to 2 ch, ** 10 ch, ss to 2 ch.

Steps 6 & 7. Into 10 ch lp work 1 dc, 1 hlf tr, 14 tr, 1 hlf tr, 1 dc. ss to 2 ch. ss in 1st dc on 10 ch lp. (4 ch, miss next st, ss in next st) eight times. (8/4 ch lps on 10 ch lp.) Ss in next 2 dc on centre ring. Repeat from ** on Step 5 to ** on Steps 6 & 7 to complete Dahlia.

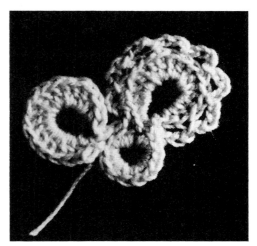

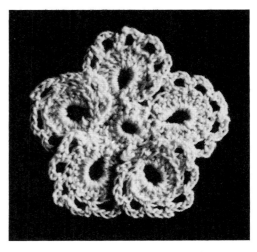

Motif 4: Ŕose 1

Original Rose Motif.

Materials:
No. 0.75 Crochet Hook.
No Padding Cord.
No. 40 Crochet Cotton.

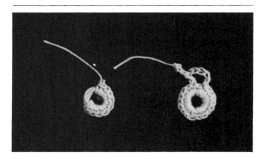

Step 1. Begin by winding cotton 10 times round No. 9 k/n. Remove from k/n, 2 ch, 17 dc into ring, ss to 2 ch.

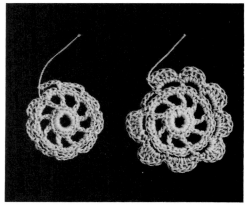

Step 6. Repeat steps 6 & 7 only work 8 ch, 1 dc, 8 tr, 1 dc in each 8 ch lp. (4 rows of petals complete.)

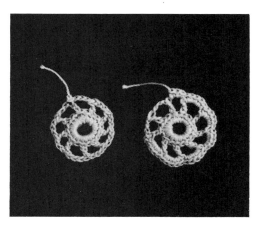

Steps 2 & 3. 5 ch, miss 1 dc, 1 tr in next dc, ** 2 ch, miss 1 dc, 1 tr in next dc. Repeat from ** to last 2 ch ss to 3rd of 5 ch. 1 ch. Into 1st lp work 4 dc, 5 dc in 2nd and each following lp. ss to 1 ch.

Step 4. ** 5 ch, miss 4 dc ss in 5th dc, repeat from ** to end of round. Into each 5 ch lp, work 1 dc, 5 tr, 1 dc, ss to back st at 1st 5 ch. (First row of petals complete.)

Step 5. Work 6 ch, ss at back of 1st petal of 1st round, repeat on round, in each 6 ch work 1 dc, 6 tr, 1 dc, (2 rows of petals). Repeat this step only with 7 ch, 1 dc, 7 tr, 1 dc, in each 7 ch lp. (3 rows of petals).

Motif 5: Rose 2

Materials:
No. 0.75 Crochet Hook
No Padding Cord.
No. 40 Crochet Cotton.

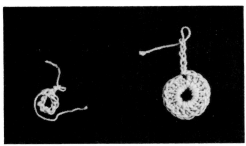

Step 1. Beg. with 8 ch, ss to 1st ch to form ring, 3 ch.

Step 2. 17 tr into ring, ss to top of 3 ch. 5 ch.

Step 3. Tr in next tr, (2 ch, tr in next tr,) 16 times. 2 ch, ss to 3rd st of 5 ch (18 sps.) 1 ch.

Step 4. 2 dc in 1st sp. (3 dc in nest sp.) 17 times, ss to 1st ch. (54 dc).

Step 5. (6 ch, miss 5 dc ss to next dc.) 8 times, (9-6 ch lps.) Over each lp work 1 dc, 6 tr, 1 dc, ss to back of 1st 6 ch petal.

Steps 6 & 7. Working into back of work, repeat step 5 twice, only on 2nd row work 7 ch, with 1 dc, 7 tr, 1 dc. On 3rd row of petals, work 8 ch, on round 1 dc, 8 tr, 1 dc.

Finishing Round. Ss into 1st dc of 1st 8 ch petal, 4 ch p in next tr, miss 1 tr, 4 ch p in next tr, (repeat twice) ss in next dc. Repeat this step on each petal. Fasten off cotton.

When commencing to crochet a chain to join in a ring, leave a short length of thread and work dc or (whatever it is) over chain and thread together. The result is a stronger ring.

33

Motif 6: Rose 3

Materials:
No. 0.75 Crochet Hook.
No Padding.
No. 40 Crochet Cotton.

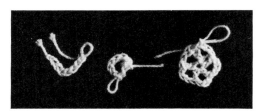

Step 1. Begin with 7 ch, 1 tr into 1st ch lp, (3 ch, 1 tr into same loop) 3 times, 3 ch, ss to 3rd of 7 ch.

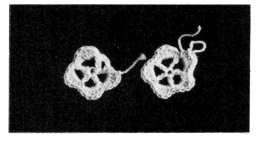

Step 2. Into each of the 5 sps, work 1 dc, 3 tr, 1 dc, (1st row of petals).

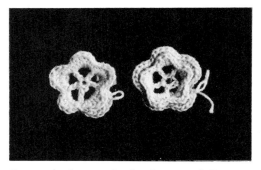

Step 3. (6 ch, ss to back of 1st petal) Repeat 4 times.

Step 4. Into each 6 ch work 1 dc, 5 tr, 1 dc. (2 rows of petals).

Step 5. (Working at back of work 8 ch, ss to back of 1st petal of 2nd row) Repeat 4 times on each petal. Into each 8 ch, work 1 dc, 7 tr, 1 dc. (3rd row of petals).

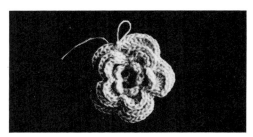

Step 6. Continue at back of work (10 ch, ss to back of 1st petal of previous round) repeat 4 times, 3 ch, 11 tr in 1st 10 ch, 12 tr in next and each remaining 10 ch, ss to 3 ch. Mesh background is worked on this round.

Step 7. DC in next tr, (2 ch, miss 1 tr 1 dc in next tr,) 5 times. Turn 2 ch, dc in next sp. (6 rows of 2 ch sps.) Cut cotton. First mesh complete.

Step 8. Miss 1 tr. Join cotton in next tr and work 2nd mesh background to correspond with first. Repeat 3 more times. Rejoin cotton between 1st and 5th mesh, work 3 dc in lps along side and round each mesh with 3 ch picots evenly spaced on round. Fasten off neatly.

Motif 7: Rose 4

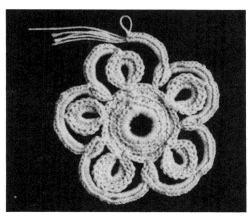

Materials:
No. 0.75 Crochet Needle.
4 Strands Padding Cotton (approx. 12″ Long.)
No. 40 Crochet Cotton.
2 Strands Padding Cotton (approx. 8″ Long.)

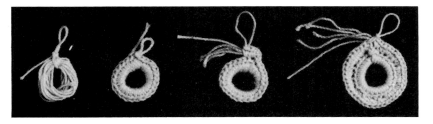

Steps 1, 2, 3 & 4. Beg. by winding p/c 15 times round 1 guage k/n, 2 ch, 25 dc into ring, ss to 2 ch. 2 ch, 2 dc in 1st dc, * 1 dc in next dc, 2 dc in next dc, * repeat from * to * on round, ss to 2 ch. (40 dc.)

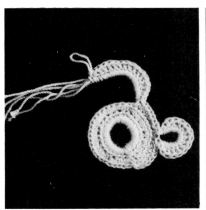 

Steps 5 & 6. B/i/p/c. Over p/c 1 dc in each next 7 dc, over p/c only 1 dc, 1 hlf tr, 13 tr, 1 hlf tr, 1 dc, ss to 7th dc. (one loop complete.) * over p/c 1 dc in each next 8 dc on ring, over p/c only 1 dc, 1 hlf tr, 13 tr, 1 hlf tr, 1 dc, ss to 8th dc. * Repeat from * to * three more times, on last loop ss to 2 ch. Fasten off p/c neatly.

Steps 7 & 8. Rejoin crochet cotton and 2 strand p/c at top centre st. of any loop, 1 ch, 20 dc over p/c only, ss in centre dc of the 8th dc on previous row, t/c, 6 dc on p/c only, ss to corresponding 6th st of last worked 20 dc, 14 dc over p/c only, ss to

centre loop, t/c. Repeat four more times. Ss to 1st st. T/C (3 ch, miss 2 dc, 1 dc in next dc) 4 times ** 3 ch, miss last 2 dc of this loop and 1st dc of next lp, (1 dc in next dc, 3 ch, miss 2 dc, 1 dc in next dc) 8 times. Repeat from ** three times, 3 ch, miss 2 dc of this lp. and 1st 2 dc of next sp. (This completes first round of mesh work.) (3 ch, 1 dc, in next sp.) Repeat all round ending with ss in 1st st.

Centrepiece. Wind p/c ten times round tip of small finger. 1 ch, 5 dc into ring. (5 ch picot, 10 dc into ring) four times, 5 dc into ring, ss to 1st ch st. Sew on centre of motif.

Motif 8: Needlepoint Motif

Materials:
No. 0.75 Crochet Needle
2 Strands Padding Cord.
(approx. 6″ long.)
No. 40 Crochet Cotton.

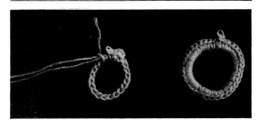

Step 1. Begin with 20 ch, ss to 1st ch to form ring. B/i/p/c, 2 ch, working over p/c, work 35 dc into ring, ss to top of 2 ch. Fasten off p/c.

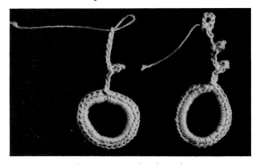

Step 2. (7 ch, ss to 3rd of 7 ch) twice, 10 ch, ss to 3rd of 10 ch. (This forms ring of floret.)

Step 3. Into floret ring, work 1 dc, 2 tr, 1 dc, (1 dc, 4 ch p.) three times, 1 dc, 2 tr, 1 dc, ss to base st of floret. (7 ch, ss to 3rd of 7 ch) twice, 3 ch, ss to 2 ch on foundation ring. 1 dc in each next 3 dc of centre ring, ss in next dc. Repeat Steps 2 & 3 eight times. (9 florets.)

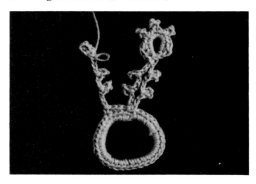

Step 4. Rejoin crochet cotton at any floret between the 2 tr (7 ch ss to 3rd of 7 ch.) twice, 3 ch, ss to between 2 tr of next floret, 4 ch, ss to opposite side of floret at back of work. Repeat until all florets are joined. Fasten off.

Step 5. Using a fine sewing needle, work a set of needle-point loops round inner circle of centre of work, using one strand of cotton for this step.

A simple collar, motifs sewn or crocheted on to a plain narrow chain band. The centre single motif shows how to arrange this step.

Motif 9: Flower

Original Old Motif, in line crochet thread.

Materials:
No. 0.75 Needle.
Approx. 30" 2-strand Padding Cord.
No. 40 Crochet Cotton.

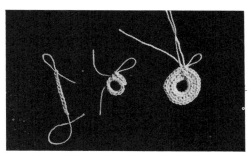

Step 1. Beg. with 10 ch, ss to 1st to form ring, 2 ch, 19 dc into ring, ss to 2 ch.

Step 2. B/i/p/c, ** over p/c work 1 dc (twice) in 1st dc on ring, 1 dc in next dc ** Repeat from ** to **, ss to 2 ch.

Step 3. * Over p/c only work 17 dc, form lp and ss to base st.

Step 4. Over p/c work 5 dc in each next 5 dc on ring, 1 dc (twice in next dc) * Repeat from * to * 4 more times. (Five loops.)

Step 5. L/p/c, 3 ch, miss 1 dc on lp, 1 tr in next dc, * 2 ch, miss 1 dc tr in next dc, * Repeat from * to * ss to base st.

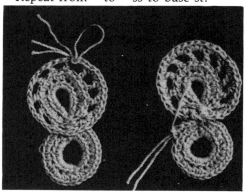

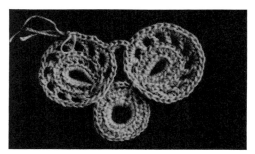

Step 6. B/i/p/c, over p/c work 3 dc in 1st 3 ch, 3 dc in next ch and each following ch, ss to base st.

Step 7. Over p/c work 1 dc in each next 6 dc of centre ring, over p/c only work 17 dc, form lp and ss to base st. Repeat Steps 4/5 until 2nd 3 ch sp. on 2nd lp, l/p/c, 3 ch, ss to corresponding 2 ch sp of 1st complete lp, 1 dc (4 times) on 3 ch, b/i/p/c, 1 dc in 2nd lp, 1 dc (three times) in each next lp on round, ss to base st. Repeat this Step working 5 complete loops with 4 dc bar joining.

Centre Raised Ring. Wind p/c 15 times round No. 1 k/n, Cut p/c and slip off needle. Join cotton, 2 ch, ** work 1 dc (5 times into ring, 4 ch, ss back to 1st dc, 1 dc (5 times) in 4 ch lp, ss in 5th dc **. Repeat from ** to ** to complete ring. Sew ring on centre of motif.

Motif 10: Shamrock

Materials:
No. 0.75 Crochet Hook.
4-Strand Cotton Padding Cord.
Approx. 12" long.
No. 40 Crochet Cotton.

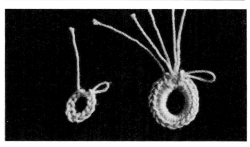

Steps 1 & 2. Beg. with 10 ch, ss to 1st ch to form ring. 2 ch, b/i/p/c, working over p/c 20 dc in ring, ss to top of 2 ch, t/p/c, 1 ch. Fasten p/c neatly. Cut p/c.

Step 3. 1 dc in each next 3 dc on ring, 4 ch p, 1 dc in each next 7 dc on ring, 4 ch p, (twice), 1 dc in each next 3 dc on ring. ss to 1 ch.

Step 4. 12 ch, (1 dc in 4th dc after picot) twice, 12 ch, ss to base of 1st 12 ch, (3 lps).

Step 5. B/i/p/c, working over p/c and 1st 12 ch lp, work 1 dc, 1 hlf tr, 2 tr, 9 d tr, 2 tr, 1 hlf tr, 1 dc, ss to base of 12 ch. Repeat this step on next 2/12 ch lps. t/c, ss to centre st between 2 lps. l/p/c.

Step 6. First leaf. ss to 1st dc, dc in 1st hlf tr, 1 ch, 1 tr in tr (twice) 1 ch, 1 tr in each d tr (9 times) 1 ch 1 tr in tr (twice) 1 ch, 1 dc in hlf tr, ss to dc, ss to centre st. (Repeat Step 6 twice) 3 leaves.

Step 7. B/i/p/c. Working over p/c 1 dc between ss and dc, 1 dc between dc and hlf tr. (2 dc 4 ch p in next sp,) 11 times, dc in remaining sps to correspond with opposite side, ss to centre st. Repeat this step on each next 2 leaves. Fasten off.

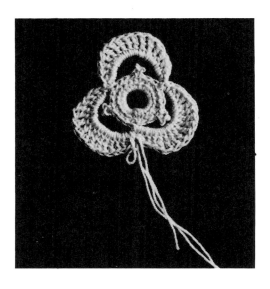

Motif 11: Shamrock Ring

Materials:
No. 0.75 Crochet Hook.
Approx. 12″ 4-Strand Padding Cord.
No. 40 Crochet Cotton.

Step 1. Begin with 10 ch, ss to 1st ch, (9 ch, ss to same place as 1st ss) twice.

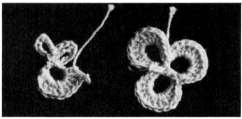

Step 2. Into each of the 3 loops, work 2 dc, 1 hlf tr, 10 tr, 1 hlf tr, 2 dc, fasten to centre leaf, 1 ch, work 1 Clones knot, 1 ch, fasten to centre by drawing thread through centre st. Cut cotton. Fasten at back.

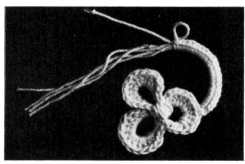

Step 3. Join cotton at centre tr of leaf (at 8th st.). Bring in p/c. Over p/c only work 20 dc, dc in centre st. of 2nd leaf. (Repeat twice more.) ss to next Leave p/c.

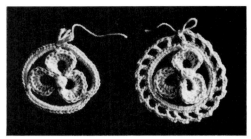

Step 4. 5 ch, miss 2 dc, 1 tr in next dc, 3 ch, miss 2 dc, 1 tr in next dc. (20 times). ss to 2nd of 5 ch. (21 lps.)

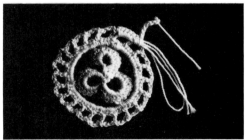

Step 5. 1 ch, bring in p/c, over p/c and in 1st lp work 2 dc, 3 dc in 2nd lp, leave p/c, 6 ch, ss this 6 ch to 1 ch on 1st lp, over this 6 ch work 2 dc 1/3 ch p, 3 times, 2 ch. (1st lp of edge complete). Repeat this step on round.

Step 6. Bring in p/c, 2 dc in 2nd lp, 4 dc in 3rd lp, L/p/c. 6 ch, ss to 1st of 2nd dc on 2nd lp. Repeat from ** on Step 5 to end of round.

Six Looped Edge. Work 5 ch, ss back into 3rd dc, repeat twice, 1 dc (3 times in 3rd 5 ch) 3 ch p, 4 dc in same lp, 7 dc in 2nd lp, 3 dc in 3rd lp, 5 ch, ss in 4th dc of 2nd lp, 5 ch, ss in 4th dc of 1st lp, over this lp work 3 dc, 3 ch p, 4 dc on same lp, 3 dc on next lp, 5 ch, ss to 4th dc of 2nd lp, over this lp work 2 dc, 1/3 ch p, repeat twice, 2 dc on same lp, 2 dc on next lp, 3 ch p, 2 dc on same lp, 1 dc on next lp, 3 ch p, 3 dc on same lp, (One 6 lp edge complete). Leave 1 dc between each edge.

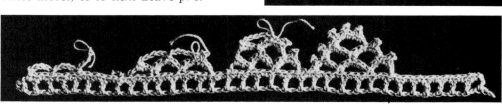

Motif 12: Three Ring Shamrock

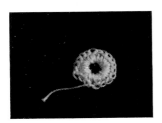

Materials:
No. 0.75 Crochet Needle.
2-Strands Cotton Padding Cord.
Approx. 14″ long.
No. 40 Crochet Cotton.

Step 1. Begin by winding C/cotton 10 times round No. 9 k/n. 2 ch, 19 dc into ring, ss to top of 2 ch, fasten off.

Step 2. Make two more rings, form a triangle by sewing rings together, finish at back of work.

Step 3. Join cotton to outside of any ring (as illustrated) 12 ch. join to corresponding outside st on 2nd ring, repeat twice, join to 1st ring.

Step 4. B/i/p/c over p/c and 12 ch lp (work 25 dc. dc to join) three times. L/c.

Step 5. (3 ch, miss 2 dc, 1 dc in next dc) 8 times, turn. ** ss in 1st sp, 3 ch, 1 dc in next sp, repeat from ** to end of row making one sp less on each row until only one sp remains.

Step 6. Leaving one st between each shamrock mesh, rejoin cotton in next st. Repeat Step 5 twice.

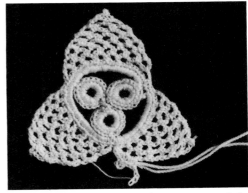

Step 7. Rejoin cotton where p/c was left, working over p/c work (3 dc, 4 ch p) in each sp round mesh leaf. Tighten or loosen p/c so that work lies flat, ss to ring. Repeat this step twice. ss to back of work. Fasten off.

Motif 13: Shamrock Scroll

Materials:
No. 0.75 Crochet Needle.
4-Strand Padding Cord.
Approx. 16″ long.
No. 40 Crochet Cotton.

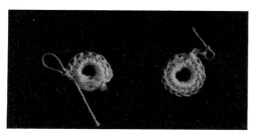

Step 1. Begin by winding cotton 10 times round No. 9 k/n. 2 ch, 14 dc into ring, ss to top of 2 ch.

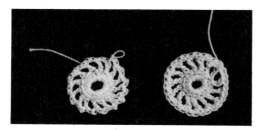

Steps 2 & 3. 5 ch, 1 tr in next dc, (2 ch, 1 tr in next dc) 13 times 2 ch, ss to 3rd of 5 ch. B/i/p/c with ss, 1 ch, work 3 dc in 1st sp. 4 dc in next and each following sp on round, ss to 1 ch.

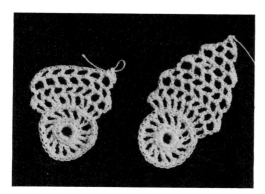

Step 4. (3 ch, miss 1 dc, 1 dc in next dc) 9 times, turn. ** ss in 1st sp (3 ch, 1 dc in next sp) to end of row, **. Repeat from ** to ** making 1 sp less each row until only 1 sp remains. Fasten off. Work 2 more matching schrolls to form shamrock.

Step 5. Rejoin cotton where p/c was left. Working over p/c work (3 dc in next sp. 4 ch p) 5 times, (3 dc in next sp) twice.

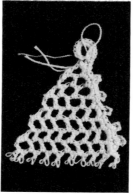  

Step 6. Working over p/c only, work 15 dc, form into ring leaving cotton and p/c at back of work. ss to 1st dc. T/c so that a nice tight ring is formed. 1 ch, 30 dc over p/c only, form a second ring outside first ring and ss to 1 ch, t/c, L/c. Working round 2nd ring ** 1 dc in next dc) 3 times, 4 ch p. Repeat from ** 8 more times, 1 dc in each next 3 dc.

Step 7. B/i/p/c, working over p/c work 3 dc in top sp, 3 dc in next sp, (4 ch p, 3 dc in next sp) 6 times, 3 dc in last sp, ss to base, ss in next dc on centre ring. Repeat Steps 4 to 7 twice more. Cut p/c. Fasten off.

Motif 14: Wheel

Materials:
No. 0.75 Hook.
4 Cotton Cord. (approx. 2½ yds. long.)
No. 40 Cotton.

 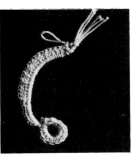 

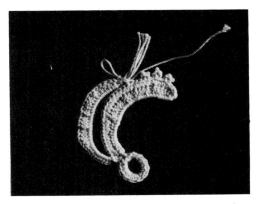

Step 1. Beg. by winding cotton 10 times round No. 6 k/n. 2 ch, 13 dc into ring, ss to top of 2 ch.

Step 2. Bring in p/c. Working over p/c, work 1 dc, 1 hlf tr, 20 tr, 1 hlf tr, 1 dc. Tighten p/c to form a slight curve. Turn.

Step 3. Working over p/c (1 dc in each of the next 2 sts, 4 ch picot) three times, 1 dc in each of the sts down spoke. 1 dc into next dc on centre ring, t/c. Turn. This completes the first spoke of wheel.

Step 4. 1 dc over p/c and into the last dc of previous spoke. Working over p/c only, 10 dc, 1 hlf tr, 20 tr, 1 hlf tr, 1 dc, ss into the 3rd dc before the 4 ch picot on last spoke. Turn. Repeat Steps 3 and 4 eleven times. On last spoke, (1 dc in each of the next 2 sts, 4 ch picot) three times, 1 dc in each of the next three sts, ss to the tip of 1st spoke of wheel. 1 dc in each of the remaining sts on last spoke, 1 dc in last dc on centre ring. Cut cord, overcast and fasten off.

Step 5. Centrepiece. Wind cotton 15 times round No. 4 k/n 2 ch, 20 dc into ring. ss to 2 ch. Fasten off and sew over centre of wheel.

Motif 15: Horse Shoe

Materials:
No. 6½ Crochet Needle.
Approx. 1½ yds. 2-Strands Padding Cord Thread.
No. 80 Linen Crochet Thread.

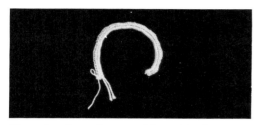

Step 1. Beg. by working 73 dc over 2-strand p/c, 1 ch, turn.

Step 2. Over p/c work 1 dc in each next 3 dc of previous row, 1 ch, turn.

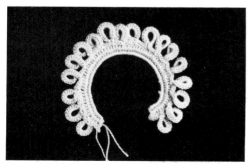

Step 3. 1 dc over p/c in each next 2 dc, over p/c only work 18 dc. Twist work to form a loop, ss to base st. ** 1 dc in each next 3 dc, over p/c only work 18 dc. Twist work to form a loop, ss to base st. ** Repeat from ** to ** 1 dc in each next 2 dc, 1 ch, turn. (18 loops).

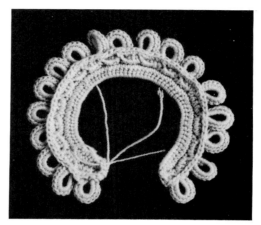

Step 4. Work 2 rows of dc into the back lps of Step 3, only on the 2nd row, increase 1 st every 4th st. (Work 2 dc in each 4th st.) to make a curve on the horse shoe. Fasten off.

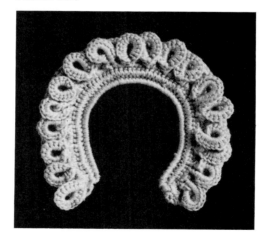

Old piece of lace with horse shoe design.

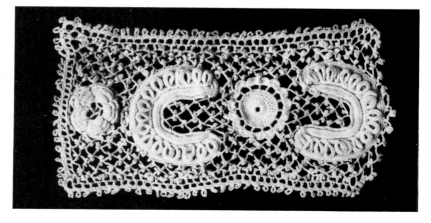

Motif 16: Cross

Materials:
No. 0.75 Crochet Hook.
4 Cotton Cord (approx. 24″ long.)
No. 40 Crochet Cotton.

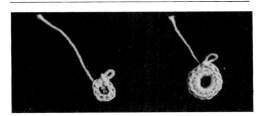

Step 1. Begin with 6 ch, ss to 1st ch to form ring.

Step 2. 1 ch, 15 dc into ring, ss to 1 ch, dc in each of next 3 sts on ring.

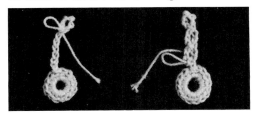

Steps 3 & 4. 12 ch, ss to 6th of 12 ch, 3 ch, 3 ch, ss to 3rd of same 12 ch, 3 ch ss to ss of Step 2. ss round base of this 3 sp loop.

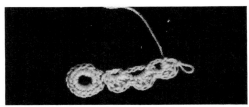

Step 5. 1 dc, 3 tr, 1 dc, in each of the first two 3 ch sps 1 dc, 3 tr, 1 dc, 3 tr, 1 dc, in 3rd (top) sp, 1 dc, 3 tr, 1 dc, in next two (corresponding) lps on opposite side. Ss to each next 3 dc on centre ring. Repeat Steps 3/4/5 three times, ending with a ss.

Step 6. B/i/p/c at centre st between any two spokes, work 20 dc over p/c only, ss to centre dc at tip of 3rd sp, over p/c only 15 dc, ss to centre dc, 17 dc over p/c, ss to centre dc, 15 dc over p/c ss to centre dc. (This forms centre lps at tip of cross.) Over p/c, work 20 dc on opposite side, ss to centre ss on ring. Repeat Step 6 three more times. ss to fasten off.

Motif 17: Shamrock Centre Motif

Materials:
No. 0.75 Crochet Needle.
4 Strand Padding Cord. Approx. 8″ long.
No. 40 Crochet Cotton.
2 Strand Padding Cord. Approx. 12″ long.

Step 1. Join crochet cotton to 4 strands of p/c, work 16 dc over p/c, ss to 1st st to form a lp, 15 dc over p/c ss to 1st ss to form a second lp, repeat second step once. (This forms 3 lps of shamrock.) t/c.

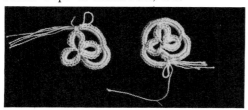

Step 2. 23 dc over p/c, dc to centre st in first 15 dc of shamrock lp, ** 14 dc over p/c, dc in centre st of 2nd shamrock lp, **. Repeat from ** to ** twice only ss last dc to 4th dc of 23 dc. t/c. (64 sts).

Step 3. 3 ch, over p/c 1 tr in next dc and each following dc on ring, ss to 3 ch. t/c. Leave p/c.

Step 4. 8 ch, ss back to 6th tr from hook, 6 dc in 8 ch, (ease 6 dc back on 8 ch,) ss to 4th dc on lp, 9 ch, ss back to 5th dc on 1st lp, 8 dc on 9 ch, 10 ch, ss back to 4th dc on 9 ch, work 12 dc over 10 ch, 4 dc over next 2nd lp and 4 dc on 1st lp, ss to base st. Fasten off. Repeat Steps 4-7 times, spacing each 3/lp group evenly.

Step 5. Join Crochet Cotton to st at side of any 3 lp group, b/i/p/c, (2 strands) 1 hlf tr, 3 tr, in 1st lp, 4 tr in 2nd lp, 12 tr in 12 dc of 3rd lp, 4 tr in 2nd lp, 3 tr, 1 hlf tr in 1st lp. To correspond with opposite side ss to next st. T/p/c. Repeat Step 5 on round.

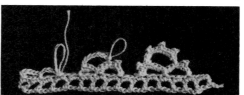

Three Loop Edge.
Step 1. Over straightening edge, work 6 ch, ss to 5th dc, (back), Repeat once, 1 dc (twice) over 1st ch, 1/3 ch p, 1 dc over ch, (3 times) ss in centre st, 1 dc in next 6 ch lp, 6 ch, ss back to 3rd dc of 1st lp, 1 dc (twice) on 3rd ch. 3 ch p, 1 dc (twice) 3 ch p, repeat once, 1 ch (twice), 1 dc on 1st lp, 1 3 ch p, 1 dc (twice). Fasten off with ss. Repeat leaving 1 dc between each edge.

Motif 18: Fern

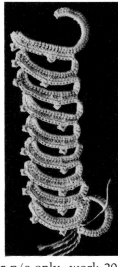

Materials:
No. 0.75 Crochet Hook
4 Strand Padding Cord. Approx. 36″ long.
No. 40 Crochet Cotton.

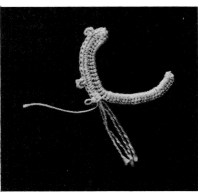

Step 1. Begin by working 46 dc over p/c, 1 ch, t/c, turn.

Step 2. Keep p/c to back of work, working over p/c 1 dc in next dc 3 dc, 4 ch p. (1 dc in next dc) 12 times, 4 ch p. (1 dc in next dc) 5 times. t/c. turn. This completes 1st frond of fern.

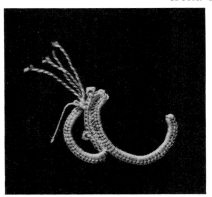

Step 3. Working over p/c only work 24 dc, t/c, 1 ch ss to 3rd st from picot on 1st frond. Turn.

Step 4. Working over p/c (1 dc in next dc) 3 times. 4 ch p. (1 dc in next dc) 12 times, 4 ch p. (1 dc in next dc,) 5 times, t/c, 1 ch, turn.

Step 5. Repeat Steps 3-4 to make the required number of fronds, only on final frond on 1st side of work after last 4 ch p work 10 dc not 5 dc as in each preceding frond worked.

Step 6. Working over p/c only, work 20 dc, ss as before, t/c, 1 ch, turn.

Step 7. (1 dc in next dc,) 3 times, 4 ch p. (1 dc in next dc) 12 times, 4 ch p. (1 dc in next dc) 5 times, (1 dc in each next dc on stem) 4 times.

Step 8. Repeat steps 3 & 4 on opposite side only, working 20 dc on p/c instead of 24 dc as on 1st row of fronds. (4 dc on 1st row are now centre stem) work 1 dc over p/c in each centre 4 dc. Ss to centre st at 1st frond. Dc in each dc on stem. t/c Fasten off.

To finish fern, fasten 2 strands p/c at centre top st of 1st stem, over 2 strands p/c work ** 1 dc 5 tr, 1 dc, fasten with ss to centre st at 2nd frond, **. Repeat from ** to ** along the centre stem. Fasten off at top frond as illustration.

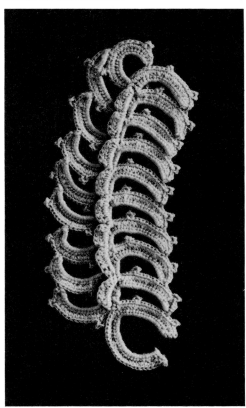

Motif 18: Sunflower

Materials:
No. 0.75 Crochet Hook.
Approx. 2½ yds 4-strand Padding Cord.
No. 40 Crochet Cotton.

Step 1. Beg. by winding cotton 10 times round No. 9 k/n. Slip off needle. 2 ch, 19 dc into ring ss to 2 ch.

Step 2. 5 ch, (1 tr in next dc, 2 ch,) 19 times, ss to 3rd of 5 ch. 2 ch.

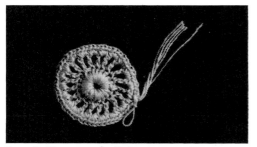

Step 3. Turn work. Bring in p/c. Over p/c, work 2 dc in 1st 2 ch sp. 3 dc in next and each following sp. ss to 2 ch. (60 sts.)

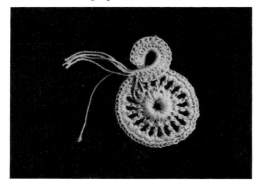

Step 4. Continue on wrong side of work. ** Over p/c only, 1 dc, 1 hlf tr, 20 tr, 1 hlf tr, 1 dc, t/c to form an even petal, twist worked petal from left to right, (as illustration) ss to base st, 1 dc in each next 4 dc **. Repeat from ** to ** (1 petal in each 4th dc.) 15 petals on 60 sts. l/p/c.

Step 5. Ss in next dc, 5 ch. ss in 2nd dc between 1st and 2nd petal (4 ch, ss between 2nd and 3rd petal) 14 times ss to 1st of 5 ch. (15 loops.)

Step 6. 3 ch, 1 tr in 1st lp, 2 ch, 1 tr in 1st lp. ** 2 ch, 1 tr in 2nd lp, 2 ch, 1 tr in 2nd lp ** Repeat from ** to ** in each 4 ch lp of previous row. ss to 1st of 3 ch. (30 loops.)

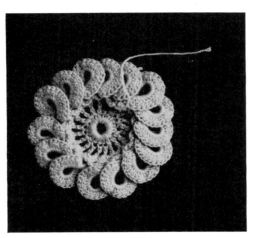

Step 7. 1 ch, turn work b/i/c, 2 dc over p/c in 1st lp, 3 dc in 2nd and each following lp on row, ss to 1 ch. (90 sts.) L/p/c.

Step 8. 3 ch, miss 1 dc (1 dc in next dc, 3 ch,) 7 times, turn. ** ss in 1st sp, 3 ch, dc in next sp, ** Repeat on each row until 1 sp remains. (7 rows). Cut cotton. Work 5 peaks same as 1st leaving 1 dc between each peak.

Step 9. Bring/i/p/c, work ** 2 dc over p/c into 1st lp. 1/3 ch p, ** repeat on round from ** to **. ss to dc between 1st and 2nd peak.

Step 10. Work 2 dc over p/c in 1st lp, 1/3 ch picot, 2 dc in 2nd lp, leave p/c, 4 ch, fasten to corresponding dc on 1st peak, 2 dc on 4 ch, 3 ch picot, 2 dc, 1 dc over p/c into loop. Continue round to finish 2nd peak. Repeat until 6 peaks are complete. Fasten 1st to 6th peak with 4 ch bar, same as before.

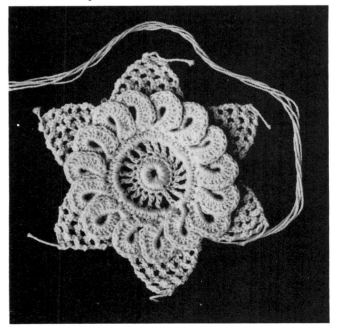

Motif 20: Shamrock and Rose Spray 1.

Materials:
No. 0.75 Hook.
4-Strand Padding Cord. Approx. 24″ long.
No. 40 Crochet Cotton.

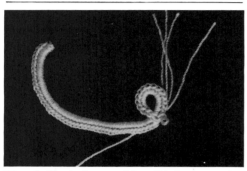

Step 1. Begin by working 84 dc over p/c. ** ss to 17th dc from hook to form ring, t/c, 1 ch. Working over p/c work 1 dc in 1st dc on ring.

Step 2. Working over p/c only, work 1 dc, 1 hlf tr, 13 tr, 1 hlf tr, 1 dc. Miss next 4 dc on ring, 1 dc in next dc, repeat twice. (3 petals)

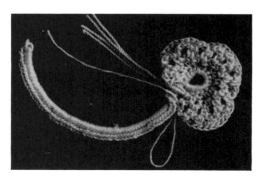

Step 3. (3 ch, 1 dc in next dc) 12 times. (This will be worked on each of the 4 dc between petals.) Turn.

Step 4. (4ch, 1 dc in 3ch lp.) 12 times.

Step 5. B/i/p/c, working over p/c, work 1 dc, 1 hlf tr, 2 tr, 1 hlf tr, 1 dc, in each of the 12/4 ch lps, t/c and arrange petals so that they lie flat. ss to 1st dc of Step 2.

Step 6. Work 3 dc over p/c only, miss first three dc of stem.(Working over p/c and in back of st on all stems), work 1 dc in each of the next 18 dc on stem.

Step 7. Work 37 dc over p/c only, repeat from ** Step 1 to ** Step 6, then 1 dc in each dc of second stem. Work 1 dc in each of the next 12 dc on first stem, Work 35 dc over p/c only.

Step 8. Repeat from ** Step 1 to ** Step 6. 1 dc in next dc down thrid stem and continue back on first stem. ss to back of petal of first shamrock rose. Cut p/c. Fasten off.

50

Motif 21: Shamrock and Rose Spray 2

Materials:
No. 0.75 Crochet Hook
4 Strand Padding Cotton. Approx. 30″ long.
No. 40 Crochet Cotton.

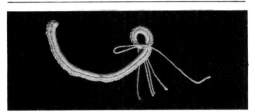

Step 1. Beg. by working 66 dc over p/c, ss to 16th dc from hook, t/c. 1 dc in next dc in next dc on ring.

Step 2. Working over p/c only, work (1 dc, 1 htr, 12 tr, 1 htr, 1 dc,) ss to 1st dc, t/c, l/c.

Step 3. 3 ch, miss 1 st, 1 tr in next st, 7 times, 3 ch, ss to 1st dc, (8 sps).

Step 4. B/i/p/c. Working over p/c, work 4 dc in each of the 8/3 ch sps. only work 1/4 ch p on every 3rd dc. This completes the 1st leaf.

Optional Centre Ring. Wind cotton 10 times round No. 9 k/n, 2 ch, 19 dc into ring, ss to 2 ch. Fasten off and sew to centre of shamrock.

Step 5. Over p/c, work 1 dc in each next 5 dc on ring. Repeat Steps 2-5.

Step 6. Repeat Steps 2-4. ss in last st on ring. This completes the Shamrock.

Step 7. Working over p/c, work 1 dc in each next 20 dc down stem. Work 35 dc over p/c only, (This forms next part of stem.) Form ring as for shamrock by ss to 16th dc from hook, t/c.

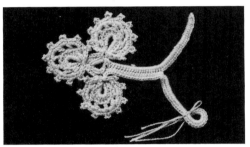

Step 8. ** Working over p/c only, work (1 dc, 1 htr, 7 tr, 1 htr, 1 dc,) 1 dc in back of 4th dc on ring. Repeat from ** twice, (1 dc, 1 htr, 7 tr, 1 htr, 1 dc,) ss to 1st dc, (Four petals.)

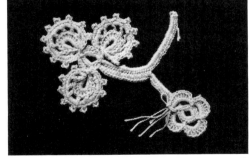

Step 9. Fold petals towards centre front and work into the 3 dc between each petal, ** 3 ch, 1 dc in 1st dc, repeat twice, ss across back of petal join, Repeat from ** to end of round. Turn. 4 ch, dc in each 3 ch lp on last round. Turn. In each 4 ch lp work 1 dc, 1 htr, 3 tr, 1 htr, 1 dc. Over p/c and in dc on rose stem, work 1 dc in each dc, continue on main stem with 1 dc in each dc to end of stem which should be nicely curved. ss to 4th p of 1st shamrock leaf.

Motif 22: Wild Rose Spray

Materials:
No. 0.75 Crochet Hook
Approx 2½ yds Padding Cotton.
No. 40 Crochet Cotton.

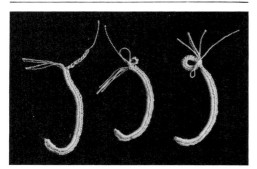

Step 1. Begin with 55 dc over p/c, t/p/c, L/p/c, ** 8 ch, ss 8th st to 55th dc on p/c to form ring. Work 17 dc into ring, ss to 1st dc.

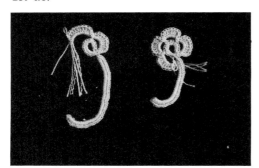

Step 2. Over p/c only work 1 dc, 1 hlf tr, 8 tr, 1 hlf tr, 1 dc, miss 3 dc on ring, ss in 4th dc, t/c to form flat petal (4 times). 1st row of petals, ss in 2 sts at back of work.

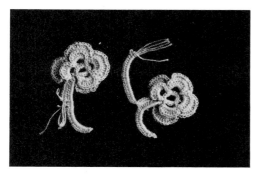

Step 3. Working at back of 1st row, over p/c only work 1 dc, 1 hlf tr, 14 tr, 1 hlf tr, 1 dc, ss in back st of 1st petal. (4 times). 2nd row of petals.

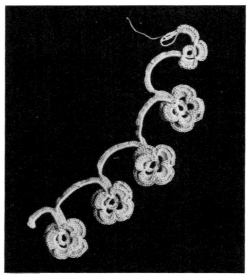

Step 4. Slip last lp to front of work, over p/c work 1 dc in each next 10 dc of 55 dc, to form stem. Over p/c only, work 45 dc, l/p/c, t/p/c, 8 ch. Repeat from ** on Step 1 to complete length of spray and no. of roses required.

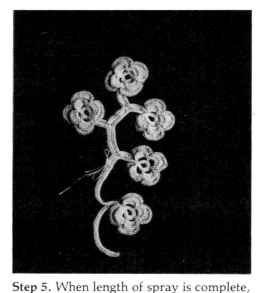

Step 5. When length of spray is complete, work one extra rose spray, which may have a longer stem (12-15) dc instead of 10 dc stem. Continue on opposite side of spray as illustration alternating rose sprays to complete spray.

Motif 23: Shamrock Spray

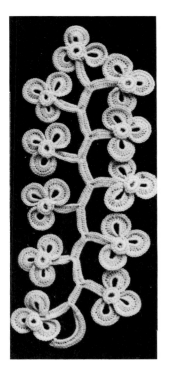

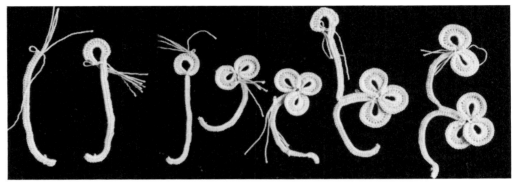

Materials:
No. 0.75 Crochet Hook.
Approx. 4 yds. Padding Cord.
No. 40 Crochet Cotton.

Steps 1 & 2. Begin by working 55 dc over p/c for stem. ** 3 dc over p/c, 1 hlf tr, 15 tr, 1 hlf tr, 3 dc, ss to 1st of 3 dc. Tighten each strand of p/c separately to form a neat loop.

Step 3. Over p/c work 1 dc in each st of previous row to complete 1st leaf. Fasten to centre 1st st. (Work 2 matching leaves)

Step 4. over p/c and into stem, work 1 dc in each next 15 dc of stem, t/c. Over p/c only, work 40 dc. Repeat from ** on Steps 2 and 3 to complete 2nd 3 leaved shamrock, work 1 dc over p/c in each next 15 dc of stem. Continue with Steps 2/3/4 to complete required length of spray. This may be only 3 shamrocks or a long spray as illustrated.

When spray is required length 3, 4, 5 or 6 shamrocks, work ** 15 dc for next stem. Repeat Steps 2/3/4 and work 15 dc over p/c on stem, work 12 dc on each next 12 dc of central stem. Over p/c only, work next shamrock with 15 dc over p/c on stem, 24 dc over p/c on central stem. Repeat from ** to finish last shamrock, continue over p/c with 1 dc in each dc of stem. (This is more difficult to work because of the length of the p/c.)

Motif 24: Rose and Shamrock Flower

Materials:
No. 0.75 Crochet Needle.
Approx. 30″ 2-Strand p/c.
No. 40 Crochet Cotton.

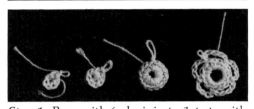

Step 1. Beg. with 6 ch, join to 1st st. with ss. 1 ch, work 14 dc in ring, ss to 1 ch.

Step 2. 5 ch, miss 1 dc, ss to 3rd dc on ring, (5 times).

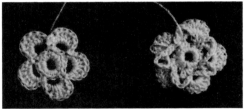

Step 3. ** dc, 1 hlf tr, 5 tr, 1 hlf tr, 1 dc, (in 1st 5 ch, ss to centre st. ** (1st petal). Repeat from ** to ** 5 petals.

Step 4. Working into back of 1st petal, work 8 ch, ss to centre st, (5 times.)

Step 5. Into each 8 ch, work 1 dc, 1 hlf tr, 8 tr, 1 hlf tr, 1 dc. (2 rows of petals complete.)

Step 6. 10 ch, ss to back of 1st petal on last row, (5 times) into each 10 ch, work 14 dc, (2 rows of 14 dc).

Step 7. ** 1 dc in 1st st. of 1st petal, ss in 2nd st, 4 ch, miss 1 dc, ss in next st, (6 times). Turn, ss in 1st 4 ch lp, 4 ch ss in next lp. ** Repeat from ** to ** until 1 lp remains. Work 4 more peaks on each remaining rose petals.

Step 8. Join 2 strand p/c at centre st between 1st and 5th mesh peak, ** over p/c work 3 dc in 1st lp, 1 4 ch p, repeat from ** in each lp at right side of peak only on final lp work 3 dc, 1/4 ch p, (twice) Continue from ** in each lp to correspond with 1st side. Over p/c only, work 1 dc, 1 hlf tr, 6 tr, 1 hlf tr, 1 dc, ss to 1st dc, (1st leaf of shamrock) 1 dc, 1 hlf tr, 8 tr, 1 hlf tr, 1 dc, ss to 1st dc and ss to centre st at base. Work 3rd leaf same as 1st. Fasten off neatly to remain flat. Continue on each peak working a small shamrock as illustration. Fasten off.

Motif 25: Marigold

Materials:
No. 40 Crochet Cotton.
Approx. 3 metres 4-strand Padding Thread.
No. 4 Crochet Needle.

Step 1. Join thread to 4 strand p/thread, 1 ch, work 50 dc over p/thread, join to 1 ch with ss to form a ring. t/p/thread.

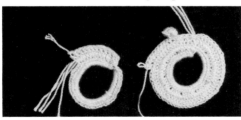

Step 2. 3 ch, over p/thread work 1 tr in bases st at 3 ch, 1 tr in each next 2 dc, 1 tr in next dc (twice.) * 1 tr in each next 4 dc, 1 tr in next dc (twice). * Repeat from * to * on round only finish with 1 tr in each last 4 dc, ss to 3 ch. (60 sts.)

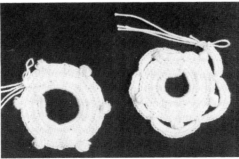

Step 3. 1 ch, l/p/c, work 1 dc in each next 5 tr of previous row, 1 ch 1 Clones Knot, * 1 dc in each next 10 tr, 1 ch 1 Clones knot, * when 6 knots are complete finish round with 1 dc in each last 4 sts. ss to 1 ch.

Step 4. * Over p/c only work 20 dc, ss to centre st between 1st and 2nd Clones knot, * work 5 more 20/dc lps, on round. (from * to *).

Steps 5 & 6. * Over p/thread and into back lps of 1st 20 dc work 1 dc, 1 hlf tr, 1 tr in each next 2 dc, 1 double tr in each next 12 dc, 1 tr in each next 2 dc, 1 hlf tr in next dc, 1 dc in next dc. T/p/thread. * (1 mitre complete.)

Repeat from * to * working 5 more Mitres. Ss in side st. Over p/thread only work 12 dc, t/p/thread, divide 4 strands and over 2 strands only work 13 dc, 3 ch, turn, miss 2 dc 1 tr in next dc, * 1 ch miss 1 dc 1 tr in next dc, *. Repeat from * to * 4 more times. (6 loops). Turn, work 5 dc in 1st lp, (at needle), 3 dc in next and each following lp, 1 dc over p/thread, turn. Over p/thread work 1 dc in each dc of previous dc row, ss to stem dc and bring 4 strands p/thread together, continue with 12 dc on 4 strands for stem and work 2nd leaf to correspond with 1st leaf worked.

Step 7. Continue with 12 dc on 4 strands p/thread for stem, divide and working on 2 strands 3rd leaf work 1 dc on 4 strand p/thread and work 2 more leaves (with 1 dc on 4 strands p/thread between each this forms a cluster of leaves.

Work on opposite side of stem with 4 strands p/thread only at opposite leaf work a matching leaf. Repeat until all leaves and stem work is finished. Sew ends neatly at back of work. Slip stitch round 1st.

* Ss in 1st 4 sts of mitre, work 1 Clones knot evenly spaced on d/treble sts, ss on remaining 4 sts of mitre. * Repeat this step on all 5 remaining mitres. From * to *. Work 1 row of needlepoint in centre of this motif.

Motif 26: Square Piece

Materials:
No. 0.75 Crochet Hook.
No. 40 Crochet Cotton.

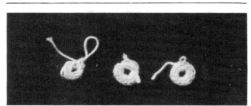

Step 1. Wind cotton 10 times round No. 10 k/n. Slip off needle and fasten cotton through to make 1 ch, work 11 dc into ring, ss to 1 ch.

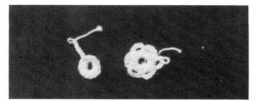

Step 2. 5 ch, miss 1 dc on ring, ss to next dc, (5 more times) 6 lps on ring.

Step 3. Work 1 dc, 4 tr, 1 dc in 1st and each following 5 lps on ring. (1st row of petals.) Bring last st to back of work.

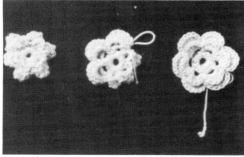

Step 4. 7 ch, ss to back of 1st petal, (repeat 5 times) work 1 dc, 7 tr, 1 dc in 1st and each following 7 ch. (2nd row of petals complete.)

Step 5. Ss in 1st and 2nd sts of 1st petal, dc in 3rd st, ** 7 ch, 4 ch p, 7 ch, 4 ch p, 3 ch, ss in 5th tr on petal, (1 complete double picot.) ** Repeat once, ss in 3rd st of 2nd petal. Repeat from ** to ** working 12 double p loops on round. Ss to centre of 1st 2 picots in 1st double picot loop. 6 ch, dc in centre of next p lp, 1 ch, turn. Work 8 dc on this 6 ch, 3 ch, turn. Work 8 tr, 3 ch ss to side st. 1 complete bar. Work 2 complete picot lps between each bar, as illustrated. (4 bars)

Step 6. On next round, work 2/2 picot loops on each 4 bars (these 2/2 picot loops are necessary to form bars on next round) with 3/3 picot loops between each 4 bars. Continue from ** to ** until size is right. (centre picot loops increasing on rounds.)

Motif 27: Rose Motif for Trimming

Materials:
No. 80 Crochet Cotton (finer if possible).
No Padding Cord.
No. 0.75 Crochet Hook.

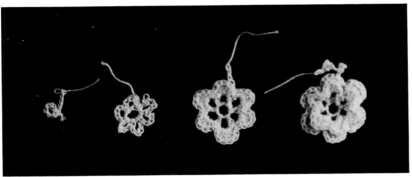

Steps 1,2,3 & 4. Beg. with 6 ch, ss to form ring. 5 ch, ss into ring, 4 ch ss into ring, (5 times) 1 dc, 1 hlf tr, 3 tr, 1 hlf tr, 1 dc, in each lp. (6 petals).

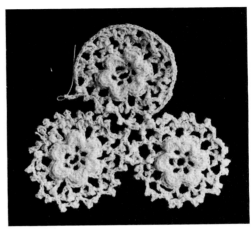

Steps 7 & 8. Work 5 ch, 3 ch p, 5 ch, 3 ch p, 2 ch, ss in 3rd st of 2nd petal. Repeat from ** on Step 6 to complete round. (12 p lps.) ss to centre p of 1st petal. Work a 2nd row of double p lps to complete this step.

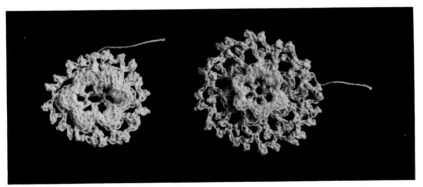

Steps 5 & 6. Work 6 ch, ss into back of 1 st petal, (6 times). Into each 6 ch lp, work 1 dc, 1 hlf tr, 4 tr, 1 hlf tr, 1 dc. (2nd row of petals). ss into 1st 3 sts of 1st petal on 2nd row. ** 5 ch, 3 ch p, 5 ch, 3 ch p, 2 ch, ss in 4th tr of petal.

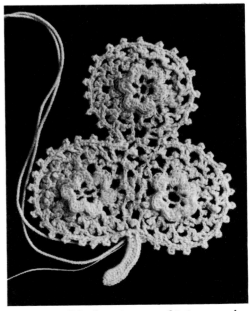

Finishing. Work 3 pieces and join to make a shamrock shape. Work 3 ch, 1 tr in centre of each two picots on outside of work. Complete this step with dc and 3 ch p. To finish, join a small double p/c and work 20 dc over p/c only. T/c. Work dc over p/c in each dc. Fasten off at back of work.

Motif 28: Mitred Fine Lace Motif
Suitable for trimming

Materials:
No. 80 Linen Lace Thread.
Approx 4" 2-strand Padding Cord.
No. 0.75 Crochet Needle.

Step 1. Over 2-strand p/c, work 2 dc, 1 hlf tr, 10 tr, 1 hlf tr, 2 dc, t/c and ss in 1st dc. Over p/c work 1 dc in each st of previous row, t/c to form a flat even leaf, ss to centre, 1 ch, work 1 Clones Knot in centre of shamrock.

Step 2. SS into 1st, 2nd and 3rd st of 1st leaf, ** 5 ch, 3 ch p, 5 ch, 3 ch p, 2 ch, ss in 3rd st, repeat twice, 5 ch, 3 ch p, 5 ch, 3 ch p, 2 ch, ss in 3rd st of 2nd leaf. Repeat from ** to complete round. (12/2p lps on round.)

Step 3. SS into centre of 1st double p, 5 ch, 3 ch p, 5 ch, 3 ch p, 2 ch, dc in centre of 2nd p. Complete 2nd round.

Step 4. SS to centre st of next p, 7 ch, dc in centre of next p. (8 times) 1 ch, turn, work 9 dc in each 8 loops. 5 ch, turn, ss in 5th of 9 dc on previous round. (16 times), turn, 4 ch, dc in 1st 5 ch lp. 4 ch dc in next lp. (15 times) Repeat two more rows.

Step 5. On last row of 4 ch lps work, in each lp, 1 dc, 1 hlf tr, 2 tr, 1 hlf tr, 1 dc, work along base 5 ch, 3 ch p, 5 ch, 3 ch p, 2 ch, to form a straightening row. Continue this row on round. Join at the side 3 double p lps with only 5 ch, 3 ch p, 2 ch, join to corresponding centre p of opposite motif.

Along the mitre edge, work 5 ch, 3 ch p, 5 ch, 3 ch p, 2 ch, ss in each mitre point. Finish with 5 ch, tr in centre of each next 2 p. Over this 5 ch, work 6 dc, tr in centre of each 2 p. Over this finishing row work a 3 lp edge.

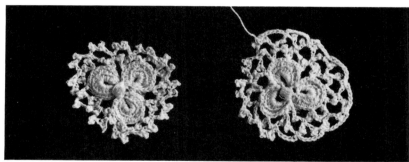

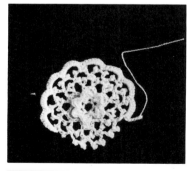
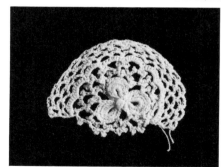

Original pieces in
the author's collection.

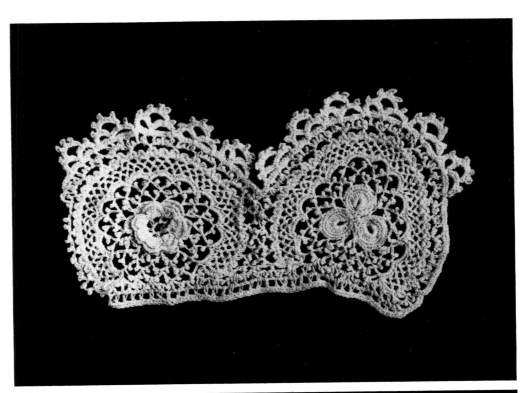

Trimming and
lawn handkerchief.

Motif 29: Vandyke Mitre No. 1

Materials:
No. 0.75 Crochet Hook.
No. 40 Cotton.

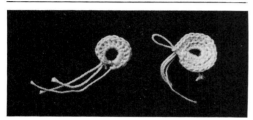

Step 1. Work as for plain square with 12/2 p loops round centre rose or shamrock.

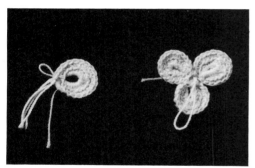

Step 2. On second row work * 6 ch bar, 1 ch, turn. 8 dc in 6 ch bar, 3 ch, turn, 1 tr (8 times) on 8 dc, 3 ch, ss in base side st. Work 2/2 picot loops * Repeat from * to * to complete 4 bars on round.

Step 3. Work 2/2 p loops on next 6 ch bar, 1/2 picot loop, 1/6 ch bar. (This to be the mitre bar, only one required.) 1/2 picot loop, 2/2 picot loops on next 6 ch bar. Repeat from * to * on round only remember to work 1 mitre bar on each alternate round.

Step 4. Work 1/6 ch bar on each 2/2 picot loops on the 4 bars already complete, on mitre bar work 2/2 picot loops. Work from * to * increasing 2/picot loops between bars until size is right.

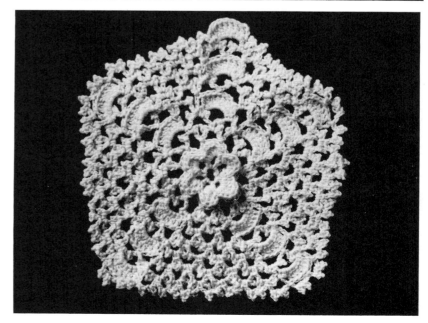

Motif 30: Vandyke Mitre No. 2

Materials:
No. 0.75 Crochet Hook.
No. 40 Crochet Cotton.

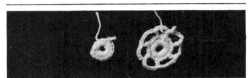

Step 1. Wind cotton 10 times round No. 9. k/n, slip off needle and fasten with a ch st, 1 ch, 1 dc (20 times) in ring, ss to 1 ch.

Step 2. 6 ch, tr into 3rd dc on ring (7 times). Into each 6 ch lp, work 1 dc, 6 tr, 1 dc. (1 row of petals complete.)

Step 3. Working in back of 1st row and at each 1st 6 ch, work 7 ch, tr into back of 1st row, (7 times) into each 7 ch lp, work 1 dc, 7 tr, 1 dc. (2nd row of petals complete.) Work a third row of petals to correspond with 2nd row only work 8 ch instead of 7 ch with 1 dc, 10 tr, 1 dc in each ch. (3 rows of petals.)

Ss into 1st 3 sts of 1st petal of last row, 5 ch, 3 ch picot, 5 ch, 3 ch picot, 2 ch, ss in 4th st of petal, work 2 p lps (16 times) on this round. (evenly spaced.)

Step 4. Ss to centre of 1st 2 picots, ch, dc in centre of next 2 picots, 1 ch, turn, work 8 dc in this ch loop, 3 ch, turn, 1 tr in each 8 dc, 3 ch, ss to base st at side and dc to centre of 2 picots. Work 4 more bars, as illustration.

Step 5 & 6. Work 1 row on next round with 2 picot lps on each bar. These 2 lps are necessary to form the foundation for the bar on next round. These 2 rows may be repeated to work whatever size is required.

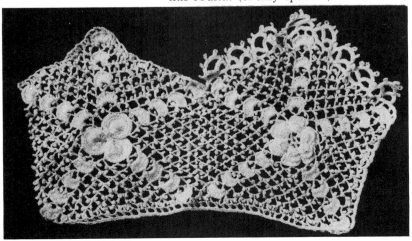

Suitable Fillings for the Backgrounds

Open Space Filling. 1 tr into place required. Work number of ch desired, 1 tr into next place required.

Single Picot Filling. 1 dc into place required, 5 ch, 1 dc into 3rd ch from hook, 2 ch, 1 dc into next place required.

Double Picot Filling. 1 dc into place required, 5 ch, 1 dc into 3rd ch from hook, 5 ch, 1 dc into 3rd ch from hook, 2 ch, 1 dc into next place required.

It is not possible to give detailed instructions for fitting the fillings and only practice will perfect this.

Filling: The motifs which make up the blouse described on p.63, arranged on the paper pattern for the garment with the filling in just begun. The filling used is double picot.

Appendix: Irish Crochet Lace Blouse

I have designed this blouse in Irish Crochet Lace for the beginner, using five motifs which are described above in the text of this book. The motifs used are:

1   Needlepoint Motif (No. 8, page 37)
2   Wheel Motif (No. 14, page 43)
3   Flower Motif (No. 9, page 38)
4   Fern Motif (No. 18, page 47)
5   Shamrock Spray (No. 11, page 40)

Making the blouse:
Instructions for even a simple garment like this can't be given stitch by stitch or row by row. This is how you go about it:

1   First of all, make the necessary number of motifs.

2   Cut a pattern in brown paper — use a dressmaking pattern as a basis (no seam allowance is needed).

3   Work a chain long enough to go around the pattern using (7ch, 3ch picot, 7 ch) repeated. Sew this chain around the edge of the shape of the pattern.

4   Place the motifs on the pattern in the desired position, taking time and care with this. When you are satisfied with the layout of the design, sew the motifs firmly in place. (You might find it helpful to have a layer of silk or lining material as well, backing the paper, for extra strength).

5   Now fill in the background, using the chain surrounding the pattern as an anchor to keep the garment in shape.

6   Do the same for the back (the design doesn't have to be the same) and stitch the back and front together — having, of course, removed the paper backing.

7   Wear it for a triumphant evening.

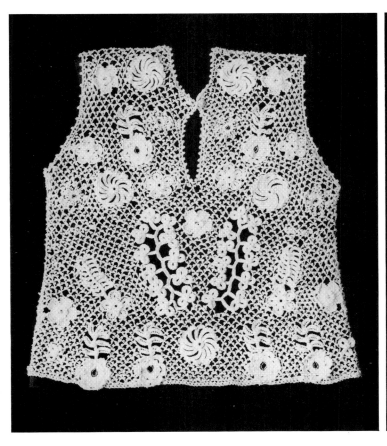